Short Story Bi

The
Unlocked
Door
and
Other
Stories

Study Guide
with Leaders Notes

By Donald L. Deffner
Earl H. Gaulke, Editor

SAINT LOUIS

Editorial assistant: Pegi Minardi

1 2 3 4 5 6 7 8 9 10   03 02 01 00 99 98 97 96 95 94

To
a very patient woman
my wife, Corrine

CONTENTS

ABOUT THIS BOOK

Everyone loves a story!

In India a native evangelist has a bicycle, a lantern, and a drum. He goes into a village, people gather at the sound of the drum, and he tells them a story. It is the story of Jesus.

Jesus Himself told stories.

> Jesus used parables to tell all these things to the crowds; he would not say a thing to them without using a parable. (Matthew 13:34 TEV)

He would say, "A certain man was going down from Jerusalem to Jericho, when robbers attacked him ..." (Luke 10:30). And a hearer mentally responded, *Yes, Rabbi, why I know just what you are talking about! Why, Uncle Daniel was attacked on that road just last week!*

Jesus followed the principle of going "from the known to the unknown." He started with the real world of his hearers and then moved on to the theological truth involved.

Stories, thus, can enliven adult Bible classes and home-discussion groups. Our involvement in the characters' lives can quicken and enrich our concern for the issue involved—pride, gossip, loneliness, witnessing, etc.—and assist us as Christians in grappling with the question (as Francis Schaeffer puts it) "How should we then live?"

The following stories are offered as an issue-oriented resource for adult Bible study and discussion groups.

There are now four courses available, each session based on 1–3 short stories, arranged topically according to thematic issues, with discussion questions referencing Bible texts designed to lead the learner to apply Scripture to his/her own life. These are for use with small home-discussion groups or in the Sunday morning or weekday church Bible class. Additionally, the study booklets can simply be used by individuals—for their own individual reading, meditation, and spiritual nourishment.

Because the story/stories for each session can be read in an average of 9 minutes (range, 5–13 minutes), the stories may be read at the time of meeting—either silently by each participant before discussion or orally by volunteer readers in the group. A third alternative is that the stories be read beforehand.

Also, the stories can be shared with people outside the church. Indeed, "tell me *your* story" can be a fruitful catalyst in reaching out to others as we first *actively listen* to *them*. My friend Christian Zimmermann, a Lutheran pastor and the flight engineer on TWA flight 847, which was hijacked some years ago, went through a lot of suffering during that hijack, but also dared to share his Christian faith with his hijackers. Christian would ask them: "What do you believe?" And they would tell him. Then he would ask: "Now, what do you think I believe as a Christian?" And they would tell him. And then he would correct their misunderstandings about the Christian faith—and share the Gospel with them.

Something else may also occur in such a dialog. As J. Russell Hale, author of *Who Are the Unchurched*, says,

> Your tone of voice, gestures, etc., are very important as you say, "I'd like to have you tell me your story about what you think of the church. Go back to your childhood." *And they really open up.*
>
> If you listen when they tell you their story, a point will come when they'll say, "Tell me your story." And you don't hand out tracts, but as the two stories converge there is the miracle of dialog, the point when *God's story* can come out . . . And the "rumor of angels" impinges on their ordinary experiences.

In whatever setting you use this book, may the Holy Spirit attend your reading. And then, may you be moved to share with others *The Story*.

Besides the discussion questions for each session, here are key questions to consider throughout the course:

1. Is the story true to life? Give reasons for your answer.
2. What, if anything, does the story have to say to our Christian faith and life?
3. How does it reveal or point to our need? (Law)
4. How does it point to or suggest God's action for us in Christ? (Gospel)

SESSION 1
Freedom

The Unlocked Door

Peter Erickson turned his greying head on his pillow. He was relaxed, contented. He stretched out his legs over the edge of the bed and took a long, deep breath. He was *very* happy.

Somewhere outside, high in the blue, an airplane droned away. Far in the distance he listened to the whistle of a lone switch engine. Beyond his window were the shouts of a baseball game, punctuated by the occasional crack of a bat.

Peter stepped to the window to watch the game. He stood squarely on the balls of his feet, his big legs spread firmly apart. He smiled. His heart sang.

What a thrill to be alive, he thought. I must be especially blessed to be so happy. So many people are distressed, grumblers. They worry about money and clothes and make elaborate plans for the future. They spend their time on the silly, shallow things. They forget simple, real values of living.

Freedom, he thought. That's most important. Freedom to think and believe as one wants. *Freedom*. He breathed the word as he said it.

If people only appreciated their freedom. It makes kings out of slaves. It turns despair into hope, a completely purposeless life into a new, challenging existence. He thrilled as he thought about freedom. It was the most important value in life. It meant everything.

His brother Ian knew what freedom meant. Ian had come from the old country with him 20 years ago. They had carved out a new life for themselves in America. They worked hard and took little time off for pleasure. Then the Depression struck, and they joined the thousands of shifting souls who moved restlessly from state to state in search of work.

Their dreams of America had not been shattered. They had started out in the West, spent 11 years working as truckers for fruit growers, and finally found security in a little business of their own.

But suddenly their life had changed. Peter, in his new-found security, began drinking. One night in a drunken stupor he ran his old truck into a farmhouse—Ian and two occupants of the house were killed.

The trial had been a nightmare. For the first time in his life Peter Erickson felt shame and guilt. They said it was manslaughter. As a result he was sentenced to 18 years in the penitentiary.

Still smiling, Peter looked out his window at the ballplayers again. The word *freedom* had taken on a totally different meaning. It was a new freedom—a spiritual freedom—from sin, from a guilty conscience, from his former life.

Yes, life for Peter Erickson was now a new man living in a new world.

When a whistle sounded in the yard, the baseball players drifted toward a tall steel gate. Peter watched them and the uniformed guard at the entrance. For a moment his thoughts wandered into the past. A shadow passed over his face and his shoulders drooped.

But not for long. He smiled and stood tall.

Freedom, he mused. My *new* freedom. Freedom to accept the fact that old things are passed away, and all things had become new. Freedom to be forgiven and begin a new life. Freedom, the most important thing in life.

Freedom Vignettes

A pastor told me about an urgent phone call he received from a man requesting an immediate visit. He went to a sleazy motel from which the man had phoned him. He told the pastor he'd been on the run from the law for seven years, for a long time hiding in a mountain cabin. He had committed only a minor offense, but had broken parole. He was riddled with guilt now and asked the pastor to go downtown and ask what the penalty would be if he turned himself in.

The pastor did so and returned to the motel. The man's wife was now with him. The pastor said he'd found out that the man's parole officer had never reported the minor offense. He was free. *He had always been free.*

Stunned and exhilarated, the man picked up his wife and danced around the room. "So I am free!" he exulted. *"Free!* I've been free all the time!"

Some people have never realized their bondage because they've never tried to get free ...

Imagine a yard where a dog is heavily chained. The dog is fast asleep and is not conscious of being fettered.

Later we see him eating his food, still chained, but since his food is close to the kennel, the chain is not bothersome. And so the dog is still not conscious of bondage.

But now the owner comes and calls the dog. The animal springs up, eager to be near his master. But he strains at the chain in vain, and now for the first time he feels the frustrating limitations of his imprisonment.

Try to get free from that which restrains you, and you will feel your bondage ...

A captive eagle was tethered to a stick by a chain 10 feet long. He marched around in a circle till a deep track was worn and years of practice confirmed the habit. At length the owner took off his chain and set him free. Still he pursued his usual circle, not claiming his freedom till someone pushed him from the beaten track.

As if astonished, he looked around, flapped his wings, then, fixing his eye on the sun, soared upward and was free ...

Once upon a time there was a man who had been in prison for 20 years but who one day walked to liberty because he tried the door and found that it was not locked.

For Discussion

1. "Freedom is really a state of mind." Do you agree? See John 8:36; Romans 6:1–11; and Galatians 2:20.

2. Freedom also involves an *awareness* and *acceptance* of our emancipation. (Not that we get "credit" for "choosing" God. He has chosen us. But our rejection of His gracious act of redemption nullifies its effect.) The parolee was no longer under condemnation, but didn't realize it. Similarly, our forgiveness and freedom in Christ took place a long time ago. How do these Scripture passages underscore that point? See Romans 8:28–30; Ephesians 1:4; 1 Peter 1:18–20; Hebrews 9:28.

3. "So if the Son sets you free, you will be free indeed" (John 8:36). As Christians, we are really like the freed eagle.

Yet we often live as if various "chains" still bind and inhibit us. What *imagined* bonds do many people still need to free themselves from? See Romans 6:9; Matthew 10:29ff; Hebrews 13:5b; Philippians 4:11; and 1 Peter 5:7.

4. Is there a "jail ministry" in your community? Is your congregation involved? What preventive measures against crime is your community involved in?

SESSION 2
Life with Others

A Neatly Ordered Life

Bettye Langley stood in front of her mirror and eyed herself. It was 8:59 a.m. She was immaculately groomed. One must keep up appearances, you know. At 59 she noticed a telltale sag here and there. But her piercing eyes, slightly flared nostrils, and elegantly raised chin offset that, and commanded people's attention.

And *respect*. Bettye had always demanded respect. That's why it was Bettye. She'd added the "e" when she was still in the eighth grade to stand out from the herd. She shook her head to ward off the painful memories of youth. It was a youth when other girls were obviously jealous of her because of her beauty, and she had few friends. But she had survived. And with her winning ways she had snagged a real catch—Bill Langley, the university senior class president.

Oh, how much she had done for him. And how carefully she had molded him over the years. He'd done well in business with her advice—and left her well off, she had to admit. Bill had died suddenly five years ago. She sighed. But she had grown to like her single life.

Bettye left the bathroom and paused in her bedroom. She eyed her bed with distaste. Bill, she'd kicked him out of that bed 15 years ago. She'd gotten tired of his reaching out to her. She still wondered how such an ugly act could

17

produce such a beautiful baby. Her heart soared. Her baby—her son—Bobby Boy. She looked at an early picture of him on the wall. That cute haircut!

Well, she had groomed Bobby Boy well, too. It was interesting what insights God had given her into other people's lives. She had chosen Bobby Boy's college for him, even gone with him for enrollment. Over the years she had wisely counselled him. The one thing she couldn't control was his wife, Rebecca. Now that woman had a mind of her own! And she and her son had had a fight just last week over the issue of Rebecca starting a business of her own.

"She should stay home and take care of you, Bobby Boy," Bettye had said sweetly.

"Mother," her son groaned. "Please don't call me 'Bobby Boy' anymore! I'm almost 40 years old!"

"Yes, I know," Bettye had said, smiling warmly. "But you'll always be my little Bobby Boy!"

Bettye turned out the light in the bedroom and headed down the stairs. She took one last look through three open bedroom doors. Each room was flawless, impeccably designed with the unique stamp of personality she had given it.

She moved down the stairs and heard a light squeak in one step. Drat! She'd hovered for hours over the last carpenter she'd hired, helping him out with pointers, and he still hadn't fixed everything right around the house. And he didn't return her calls anymore. It was so hard to get decent help these days. People in that class were *so* irresponsible.

Bettye's foot touched the first floor, and she walked several steps to the front door and opened it. Her tree roses were blooming nicely, she noticed. She picked up the morning paper and headed back for the kitchen.

Passing through the dining room she checked on the table. She had her finest silver and china laid out in four place settings. Always ready for guests, she proudly complimented herself. And always ready to be admired by those who could discern her fine taste for things.

And on into the kitchen. There were the two pecan pies she'd gotten up early to bake. They would surely take the prize again at the Ladies' Aid benefit social tonight. Her generous contributions to all their special projects would assure that, she mused wryly—as would her periodic checks to Rev. Nussbaum, which would keep him preaching the inoffensive kind of sermons she liked to hear.

Bettye walked out to the breakfast nook and peered into the backyard. All tidied up. In fact, her life was tidied up. She harrumphed a sigh of satisfaction and headed for her favorite chair in the sunroom just off the breakfast nook.

Sitting regally in her chair she took stock. All set for the social tonight. House in order. Life in order. If only other people had her insights—could see things the way she did. If they just had her understanding, and the perception she had to make decisions, and as clearly as she always did.

All I have to do is *tell* them, she mused wisely, and they should understand.

Well, it's been some time since Bobby Boy has phoned. Of course he'll call today. And someone will want to know how to arrange the flowers on the tables tonight. They'll phone. I have some good ideas on that. They'll welcome my advice. And Pastor just might drop by.

Bettye shifted to a comfortable position in her chair and rearranged a small vase of flowers. She placed the phone at her left elbow and sat back expectantly.

Surely someone would call or drop by. They would need her guidance on something.

But the phone did not ring that morning. And no one came to call.

For Discussion

1. How do you evaluate the world-view of Bettye Langley?

2. What can you say in her defense? Doesn't her approach to life and her relationship with other people seem totally logical to her?

3. Do you see part of yourself in Bettye Langley? In what way? In what ways are your attitudes toward other people justified and in what ways do you think you should change? See 1 Corinthians 10:12.

4. Anne Morrow Lindbergh said, "Him that I love I wish to be *free*—even from me!" Why don't we truly free others? If we don't free them, doesn't that mean we don't really love them?

5. Read the "Chapter on Love," 1 Corinthians 13, in the following version. After each verse, pause and examine how it can be applied in our daily lives. Try to illustrate how we fail to fulfill the apostle's instruction. Then suggest specific ways in which we, motivated by the Holy Spirit, might "practice what we preach" (vv. 1–2).

> I may be able to speak the languages of men and even of angels, but if I have no love, my speech is no more than a noisy gong or a clanging bell. ²I may have the gift of inspired preaching; I may have all knowledge and understand all secrets; I may have all the faith needed to move mountains—but if I have no love, I am nothing. ³I may give away everything I have, and even give up my body to be burned—but if I have no love, this does me no good. ⁴Love is patient and kind; it is not jealous or conceited or proud; ⁵love is not ill-mannered or selfish or irritable; love does not keep a record of wrongs; ⁶love is not happy with evil, but is happy with the truth. ⁷Love never gives up and its faith, hope, and patience never fail.

⁸Love is eternal. There are inspired messages, but they are temporary; there are gifts of speaking, in strange tongues, but they will cease; there is knowledge, but it will pass. ⁹For our gifts of knowledge and of inspired messages are only partial; ¹⁰but when what is perfect comes, then what is partial will disappear.

¹¹When I was a child, my speech, feelings, and thinking were all those of a child; now that I am a man, I have no more use for childish ways. ¹²What we see now is like the dim image in a mirror; then we shall see face-to-face. What I know now is only partial; then it will be complete—as complete as God's knowledge of me. ¹³Meanwhile these three remain: faith, hope and, love; and the greatest of these is love. (TEV)

6. Study Philippians 2:1–11. What particular message is there that speaks to the "selfish self" in each of us? How does the Gospel in the latter verses apply to all of this?

A Glad Heart

So Amy Lawson had retired after teaching parochial school for 40 years. She eyed the small glass of paw paw wine in her left had. No ring on that hand.

"The wine that maketh glad the heart of man." Well, not *her* heart. She looked around her modestly furnished apartment. There was the plaque the congregation had given her four months ago at her retirement dinner. It *had* been a joyous occasion. And people were so grateful and gracious to her. A trip to Europe whenever she wanted it. And a new Jeep Station Wagon—her favorite kind of car.

21

She had been overwhelmed. But that was in May. It seemed so long ago. She'd spent the summer with relatives in Seattle. And now she was back in her little town of Dowagiac, Michigan. But no classes this September—for the first time in four decades!

She had slept in this morning, still exhausted from her trip—and, the last school year! Once she heard the nearby parochial school bells ring. But not for her. She'd turned over and gone to sleep again.

She looked back over the years. She could remember when a single stove heated the first one-room school. She'd put a pan of water on top of the stove to balance the humidity. *She* shoveled the coal. Other smells came back to her—stale sandwiches, rancid lockers, soiled sports clothes.

Winters in Michigan had been the toughest. She remembered pulling boots on the tiny feet of 20 young children several times a day. Once the last child said, "These aren't my boots." Amy had laboriously taken off the boots. "Where *are* your boots?" She asked. The child responded, "These aren't my boots. They're my *brother's*. But my mother makes me wear them." And Amy pulled the boots back on again.

But the congregation improved conditions at the school, in fact, put up a new one a few years later. But her salary hadn't gone up. And so she'd lived somewhat meagerly over the years.

And, at times she had been lonely. "Just down a little," she preferred to tell herself. For she always distinguished between lonely and being alone. Her parents had died years ago. And so early on she had learned the blessings of solitude. Loneliness was never a pit for her. But solitude was a well of strength—quiet hours in reading and in prayer. She dwelt on her confirmation verse: Hebrews 13:5 "I will never leave thee, nor forsake thee." To hell, then, with self-pity, she affirmed, quoting Elizabeth Elliott, one of her favorite authors.

And getting her mind off herself, she threw all of her energy into her teaching—which she loved. And toward other people—for whom she had such affection. She was a person of complete commitment and self-confidence in what she did. She was absolutely absorbed with the total life of her children at school. And when Amy was elsewhere with other friends she always gave each individual her concentrated attention.

For example, if she was talking to you, she looked right into your eyes. She never looked over your shoulder to see if there was someone else she'd rather talk to. And if she was driving you somewhere, when she came to a stop sign, she would keep talking—or listening—to you until the car behind honked at her, so concerned she was in giving you her undivided attention.

And Amy was a very *caring* person. She often said, "Are you *sure?*"—in offering someone more food, or a ride, or other help. People would just smile nicely at her and respond politely.

Except once at a party she said, "Are you *sure?*" And the person replied rudely, *"I told you, 'NO THANKS!', didn't I?"* But Amy was self-confident. And without skipping a beat, she simply remarked, "I was just offering ... just wanted to be of help," and the conversation went on.

Maybe her self-confidence had intimidated some of the men she'd met. But Amy doubted that. Oh, she would have gotten married. That is, if "Mr. Right" had ever come along. She recalled a novel she'd once read about a flyer going down in his plane during the war. Something like, *Never again would he feel the soft touch of a woman. Never again would he feel her warm body against his own.*

She would *never* have that experience ... holding a man she could love and care for and give herself to. *That* blessed intimacy was a gift from God to *other* people, not to her. It was denied her. She accepted that. She didn't like it. But she didn't resent it. The life she had was what God had called her to.

Amy looked at the clock, 11:30 a.m. Better get some food in the house. And so, after a light lunch, she got into her Jeep and headed for town.

Most of Dowagiac's shopping area was within several blocks. And as she went from the bank to the grocery store she began bumping into one friend after another.

"Timmy's really missed you this summer," said Mrs. Barnes. "He couldn't *wait* for you to get back! We didn't know exactly when you'd return. Look, we're having a barbecue tomorrow—*Friday* night. Can you come? *Please?*"

Amy agreed and after a few more bits of conversation continued to carry packages to her car. "Amy!" yelled Al Wiggins, a co-teacher. "Where have you *been?!* We've all missed you! Look, Saturday afternoon, a softball game at school and a swim afterwards. Will you come?"

And so it went, on and on. It took *three hours* to get her errands done. One after another of her pupils, their parents, friends from church—she even bumped into the pastor and his two boys—embraced her, hugged her, made her promise to come to a dinner, or a game, or some other event.

Eventually Amy got home, exhausted. But it was an exhilarating kind of exhaustion this time. She put all her purchases away, rested a bit, and then got into her Jeep again and headed for her favorite restaurant on the edge of town.

She walked into the place and took a quiet corner table. But it wasn't quiet for long. Amy just couldn't believe it. Person after person saw her and came over and started inviting her to things. Time and time again parents told her how much she had done for their children. In one family eight children had been in her classes for over 23 years. She didn't get out of the restaurant for two hours.

Finally she got home again. It had been *some* day. She put on *Eine Kleine Nachtmusik* and sat in her favorite chair by the fake fireplace.

Just one little glass of wine before going to bed.

"*So I am* not *alone,*" she mused "*I do* have *a glad heart, after all. But the wine hasn't done it. God has given me a full life. God—and His children. My "children"—of 40 years.*

Amy picked up her datebook and the scribbled notes she'd been making all day. As she filled in the spaces a smile slowly spread across her face.

For Discussion

1. How do you feel Amy is handling the new chapter in her life?

2. Do you think Amy's personality was a little "strange"? Why or why not?

3. What does 1 Corinthians 12 have to say about differing personalities? Romans 12?

4. Does God really "call" a person to single life? See 1 Timothy 5:14. Do Paul's words to Timothy mandate marriage? (See also 1 Corinthians 7:7ff.)

5. What is the difference between loneliness and solitude? Are you a "solitude" person? How does one *avoid* loneliness but *find* solitude?

SESSION 3
Communication

Don't You Like My Present?

He closed the hotel room door behind him softly. It had an ornate, carved handle—this heavy old door which led to their room in the quaint little hotel in the small village high in the Swiss Alps. Inside were two fluffy beds with massive down pillows. Comfortable, cushioned chairs were in each corner. A conveniently placed buzzer kept a maid or bellboy only a few seconds away. And through the windows—ah, through the windows!—one could see the majestic snow-covered peaks rising above the meadows beyond the village square.

Slanting his video camera down from his window into the hotel garden, he had gotten a shot of Eunice languishing on a bright white wooden-slatted bench. Then he had taken a view of her from below, as she stood on the small balcony outside their room, surrounded by a chorus of boxed and potted flowers, chiming together with their dazzling colors.

He could hear his friends laughing now—once they showed the video when they got back to the States in three weeks—and saying, "You must have run down those steps awfully fast to get those pictures, Chris!"

But he wasn't laughing now. And as he walked slowly down the carpeted hall away from the room, he had the sinking feeling of being alone—terribly alone—even though he was with Eunice in the very place where he thought they would, perhaps, find so much happiness together again.

The jolting memory of something that had happened months ago, early one morning on the way to work, snapped into focus in his mind. It seemed sad, tragic, unbelievable then. He had picked up a nodding acquaintance in the car pool at 7 a.m., and as the man squeezed himself into the front seat with another passenger in the seat alongside Chris, he heard him mutter with a deep sigh: "Wow! It's a relief to get out of that house again!"

And as his fellow workers in the car questioned him with somewhat halting but curious comments, Chris heard the man spell out the story of a hollow life that saw nothing but misery and hate and bickering in his home. He was a man who lived only for the time that he was out of the house, away, far away, from his wife, with other men, with anyone else, as long as he felt just a little free from the drab prison cell that his marriage had become.

But now, to his own gradual and utter amazement, *he* had begun to feel the same way. The happy planning for the long-awaited European trip, the festive bon voyage party, the exciting new days aboard ship, and then, as their stomachs settled, the first few days on the Continent—all these were in the past. And here he was, with a wife of nine years, everything he had thought he could ever wish for in a woman. And yet his most constant companion, instead of this ideal, this *dream* he had thought she would be, his hourly companion, had become—not his wife but a numbing, heart-wrenching mistress called Loneliness.

It was strange to him how there could be such loneliness *in* married life. He had thought the years *before* the distant wedding day had been painful enough—the years in school, spending whole evenings over the books, rarely dating even the fair young women who had cast hopeful glances his way; the two dreary years in the Army; and then the frustrating several years in his job at the office, before he finally took the leap and asked Eunice, whose desk was next to his, to marry him.

And he wondered what had happened to her over these nine years. He didn't want to blame her for what he felt they had lost. It wasn't that they hadn't any children, either. Not that it wouldn't have changed things—perhaps a great deal. But somehow they both understood that it just hadn't been in God's plan up to this time that they have any, much as they kept hoping they could.

No, it was something, something that went far deeper.

Approaching Chris, coming down the wide hallway (almost a long parlor in itself), came the elderly couple he had seen several times on his floor of the hotel. They nodded to him, almost bubbling over with smiles and bows, as they bustled on by him to their room. Chris neared the ancient, metal-cage elevator, and pushed the button.

No, he mused, it was something deeper and more profound that they had lost in their marriage. He suppressed what felt like a justifiable welling up of anger and decided instead on a calm, reasoned decision that it was Eunice's plain *coldness* that had destroyed whatever spark of love and bond of life that had ever been between them.

He actually wanted so little, he thought, as he heard the slow, steady whine of the elevator, bringing it up to his floor. Warmth, affection, not just physical response, but *little* things—like reaching out to adjust his tie, or taking his arm when they crossed the street, or touching him ever so lightly when they passed each other in a room.

Crazy? He didn't think so. So she *was* tired, drained from the trip, the boat, the cabs, the trains, the late hours. Somehow, though, it seemed he didn't have a wife anymore, even though they had shared bed and board for these nine years. He was married, had a good job, no financial worries, and here he was on a ball of a vacation. But he was sick with tiredness of being married but nevertheless terribly, achingly, alone.

The elevator arrived, and he rattled the door of the cage open and stepped inside. In a few moments he was in the lobby of the building. After a quick glance behind the registry desk at an empty letter box marked 406, he stepped out into the cool mountain air. A few people were on the small winding street, and he looked up it, beyond the shops and gables to the purples and whites of the mountain peaks again. Somehow he never tired of just gazing at them.

Here and there the people glided past on their bicycles, and in the distance, a block away, he could see them straining as they pedaled up a sharp rise on the street that led to the outskirts of the village.

He glanced quickly up to the room he had just left. Eunice was sleeping now. She would be sleeping for two hours at least. She had calmed his light, earlier mood with a few quick comments that she was going to get some rest. And she had pulled off her shoes, put on her dressing gown, stretched out on the bed, and promptly shut him out of her world by closing her eyes.

He moved on in his private world now, walking alone in the middle of the passing townsfolk and cyclists and occasional small foreign cars.

"*Foreign* cars." Ha! They weren't "foreign" over here! In Switzerland you could get anything you wanted to rent, not for a particularly modest cost, of course. But he had said, "Hang the cost": he was going to drive something on those mountain roads he felt safe in. And so they had rented a heavier car than the lightweight compact cars, a four-door Audi.

He headed for the garage, where they had left the car the night before, and after a few moments of greeting the attendant in fractured German he steered the automobile out of the garage and up the main street toward the outskirts of town.

He mentally came to a paragraph in his introspection as the mechanical reflexes of driving absorbed his hands and feet. He would see Eunice later. Maybe he would talk to her. Maybe ... maybe tonight ... or tomorrow ... maybe she would feel different. Yes, he'd talk to her again. But for now he was going to drive and enjoy just being a part of the high, picturesque world he saw gliding before his eyes through the windshield.

And then, suddenly, his foot had jammed on the brakes with a slam, involuntarily, before he had sent the message to it. He heard a scream, a heavy bump as a boy on his bicycle almost flew into the front end of the heavy car, and an even more sickening thud as the front wheel locked onto the bicycle's wheels and ground to a halt.

Deep in the pit of his stomach Chris felt as he had so often on the ship. Then came a wave of fear, followed by a horror of even getting out of the car to look at what happened. But, steeling himself, he locked the gears of the car into "park" so as not to back over the body of the boy, wrenched the emergency brake on, and stepped out the door.

Underneath the right front wheel of the heavy car was the bicycle, the round circle of the front wheel twisted into a broken pretzel shape, the seat of the bicycle bent awry, the other wheel out of sight underneath the frame of the automobile.

And limping around on one foot was the boy, a lad of 12 with blond, close-cropped hair, rubbing his right leg, and yelling over and over again, in his strange sounding Swiss German, something like "ya' shoulda watched where you were going!"

Overwhelmed with relief that it was the bike and not the boy which lay mangled under the heavy tire. Chris walked up to him and asked, "Are you hurt?"—a stupid question, as he immediately agreed. He also rapidly assured the lad that he would get a new bike, yes, a new bike. "Don't worry about that a bit," he told him.

The boy's leg was badly scraped. Actually he had not hit the car, but jumped clear as his bike went under the car. In hitting the pavement he had scraped the flesh of one leg and also earned a slight scratch on one elbow. But beyond this he was unharmed.

The ensuing drama was one which went by slowly, and yet, as if in a dream, Chris seemed to watch it from the distance as a spectator. A policeman was on the scene almost immediately. Chris didn't like to think of the legal complications, insurance matters, and other delays which might come from the accident, especially considering the fact that he and Eunice had hotel bookings all the way up the Rhine for the next three weeks.

He decided to take events one by one as they came. Talking quietly and consolingly to the boy, Chris watched the policeman as he, soon joined by another officer, began questioning bystanders. The boy had stopped limping now, and he kept reassuring Chris that he was all right. Even the bike had strangely enough been bent back into reasonable shape by the strong arms of a hefty fellow who had joined the crowd of villagers who had gathered after the accident.

Finally, the policeman came over to Chris, and after slowly and deliberately examining his international driver's license, he respectfully announced to Chris that the witnesses had all agreed that the boy had been at fault and had not yielded the right of way to the driver of the car. Indeed, said the officer, the boy could be prosecuted for improper operation of a cycle! And the laws were very stringent on this in his village, he assured the American stranger.

The villagers gradually dispersed after the officers finished speaking to Chris, and the boy finally left, too. Toward the end of the little incident it seemed that the boy was more intrigued by his involvement with the officers than by the accident itself. The boy did not leave, however, without Chris pressing a handful of francs into his hand to take care of the damaged bicycle.

Finally, Chris climbed back into the auto and headed away from the intersection, shuddering as he went. Within a block he pulled the car over to the curb, and walking to the edge of an alley he leaned against the side of the wall and shook uncontrollably.

A half hour later, far out in the country, some mental pieces of a jigsaw puzzle began to form themselves together in his mind. He realized now that for days he had been silently praying to God to help him with his problem with Eunice, to lead him to understand her, or better, to move her to show some warmth and affection for him, so that he might somehow shake off the brooding, aching hours of loneliness that filled his life.

He hadn't really *said* the words to himself. And yet they had been there—deep in his subconscious. "O Lord, give me a sign!"

And, now, strangely, in a way he would never have suspected, he *had* a sign. It wasn't a sign that involved Eunice at all, really. And yet it did, too. Plagued by the fright of that moment when he had feared to step out of his automobile and look beneath the wheels of the car, Chris tried to imagine what it would have been like if he had killed the boy— even if the boy had been at fault in barreling into the side of the car. He tried to imagine what his days and months would have been like *if that boy had died*—and he would have had to live with the memory of that death in his mind until the casket was closed for himself.

Suddenly, over and over again, came a rush of *"thank God"* as he tried to rid his mind of the horror that could have followed the brief accident at the intersection back in the small village. Even if the boy had lived, but had been crippled for life, what an agonizing sense of guilt he would have had!

Chris forced the thoughts out of his mind and began the reasoned process that started to bring an increasing sense of peace back into his being.

God had given him a sign, a strange kind of sign. It wasn't just a simplistic formula of "count your blessings" either. It was a much deeper realization that Chris really had so much to be thankful for, that maybe he was feeling too sorry for himself to realize what good gifts God had already given him in his life.

Somehow it had taken the strange shock of a bicycle-auto accident to jolt him into thinking this way, but it all started to make sense. *Life* started to make sense. After all, he began to think, we've been together for nine years now, Eunice and I. *God* gave us those years, and He must have given us something memorable to be together that long and share what we have shared together.

He looked out over the calm, green meadows of the Alpine valleys that stretched before him, and the distant yellow-white peaks that lay far ahead of the car. Maybe he should take Eunice for what she was. God had given her to him. She was sort of God's *present* to him. Goodness knows, *he* was no prize himself.

And then he remembered it—a trifling little incident that had happened years ago at some neighborhood birthday party he had attended. He had been only a spectator to the drama, but had never forgotten the hurt, crushed look on a little 8-year-old's face when something happened at that party.

She was a neighborhood playmate of his, and another girl from a rather well-to-do home had invited them, together with about 10 of the neighborhood kids, to her well-appointed home for her birthday celebration.

The 8-year-old girl had always liked the little "rich girl" (as they called her) and had gone to some considerable piggy bank expense to select a present for her more affluent playmate. What the gift had been, Chris couldn't now remember. A trinket of some kind. But whatever it was, the other moppet had taken one look at it, and with a disdainful toss of her head, thrown it onto the couch and walked back to her other presents.

"But I picked it out *just for you!*" he could still hear the crushed little girl cry after her.

And he still remembered how she had followed the lass with the disdainful air across the room and then asked wonderingly, almost beseechingly, "Don't you like my present?"

For Discussion

1. What do you feel is the *real* source of Chris's loneliness?

2. What do you think of the comment, "I think Chris's solution to the problem is just a matter of 'putting up with a bad situation' "?

3. At one point Chris wondered if he was "feeling too sorry for himself." Elizabeth Elliott has said "to hell with self-pity." Catherine Marshall speaks of how a degree of self-pity can join the blown-up pride of our self-congratulation at having been so patient and reliable with other people and calls the mixture a "deadly brew" (*Something More,* p. 137). Author Hannah Smith said, "All discouragement is of the devil." What does Scripture have to say about all

this? See Genesis 50:20; Matthew 6:25, 32; 1 Peter 5:7; 2
Corinthians 12:9–10.

4. What can lead to the loss of intimacy in a marriage? In
   this story what do you think were the key factors?

5. The story spoke of "viewing one's spouse as a *present* from
   God." In what ways could that perspective change an otherwise humdrum or perfunctory relationship?

6. Whether you are single or married, what do you look for
   most in making a friend or seeking a life partner? See
   John 15:13; Romans 12:9–10. Also Ephesians 5:21, 22, 25;
   1 Peter 3:1–2, 7–9.

SESSION 4
Self-Awareness

The Ugliest Face He'd Ever Seen

"Big Bill" Reiker settled down in his airline seat and scrutinized the boarding passengers. He always got on before the others, claiming he had a "bad hip." Then he would shuffle onto the plane. Trouble was, he forgot to shuffle when he got off.

With distaste he noticed the characteristics of those who would be his fellow passengers for the next several hours. Just ahead of him were three loud-mouthed businessmen braying about their latest "deals." He *hated* their arrogance.

An old man, white hair awry, came down the aisle and smiled at Bill. There was gold in his teeth. Bill turned away.

"Oh, no!" Bill groaned. To his left a person opened a deck of cards. "The Card Shuffler" was aboard! He abhorred that traveler with a vengeance. The person would split the deck, pound each half on the tray table, then split the cards together endlessly. Crack! Crack! Crack! Split! Split! Split! There oughta be a law!

"Everything all right, sir?" the hostess beamed at him. Bill grunted. He resented people who were always cheerful.

And on the other passengers came: the screaming babies,

tittering teenagers, bald men and old women with lined faces, searching for their seat numbers. They limped as they looked. Why weren't they home in rocking chairs? he mused.

Three times bags smashed his hand on the armrest. One woman's purse banged him on the head.

"Sorry!" she smiled. Bill set his jaw. Par for the course.

Now "The Paper Rustler" began. The man seated next to him opened wide his *New York Times* and after only a quick glance at each page turned-folded, turned-folded the paper endlessly. Disgusting!

Bill closed his eyes as the flight attendant's standard harangue on the P.A. began.

"Take out your folder ... follow along ... fasten your seat belt this way." Finally they were airborne.

Bill's stomach growled. When will they ever bring the drinks? After a seemingly endless delay the chattering flight attendants began to roll the drink cart down the aisle.

"Ouch!" Bill yelled, as the cart hit his elbow.

"Sorry!" the flight attendant grinned.

The man ahead of him pushed his seat all the way back. How thoughtless! Bill shifted uncomfortably.

Finally, *finally* the drink cart reappeared.

"What'll you have, sir? the attendant asked pleasantly.

"Two whiskey sours," Bill said acidly. He paid the woman, and soon had gulped one down.

Well now, there, he thought. Maybe I can make it through the flight after all. And Doreen would be meeting him. Sweet daughter Doreen. Since Dorothy, his wife, had died, Bill flew east to see her every few months.

Sweet Doreen. There was a real Daddy's girl if you ever saw one. Loving. Accepting. Knew him for what he was. A successful, *very* successful businessman. Bill settled back in his seat and reached for his second drink.

The liquor was calming him down nicely, he thought. And, well, in my usual affable way, I should at least be polite to my seatmate. The man had put his *New York Times* down now and was nursing a Coke.

"Fly very much?" Bill asked brightly.

"Yes," the man responded, "I'm an engineer, and ..."

"Well," Bill warmed to the occasion. "I am, too. Built every bridge overpass between Fairfield and Sacramento!"

And he raised his voice gradually so the businessmen in the seats ahead could have the benefit of his revelations.

The conversation went on for about 10 minutes, or rather, the monologue, as Bill traced his engineering career from its beginning and brought the man up to date on his latest achievements.

"Your dinner, sir." The attendant handed a tray past Bill to his seatmate and he immediately began eating.

"None for me, Miss," Bill said crisply, "I'll have another whiskey sour."

Bill looked around. Most passengers were absorbed in their meals now. He reached for an airline magazine and began flipping the pages loudly. "*Ahh,*" he sighed, and pushed his seat all the way back.

Ahead of him stretched the bald heads, the white heads, the ... Bill had to go to the bathroom.

Extricating himself from his seat, he jerked down the aisle. A small pain made itself known in his hip. He limped to offset it, and quickly ignored it.

In the restroom, he flushed the toilet, rinsed his hands, and then caught his image in the mirror. The ruins of a once handsome face glared back at him. Bill's jaw opened slightly in disbelief. A glint of gold showed in his teeth. His hair was frizzy around a perfectly bald pate. Suddenly a vignette he'd just read in the airline magazine came to mind.

It was about a man who had rushed up to a subway ticket booth and slapped a coin down on the counter. When he didn't immediately get the change coming to him, he looked to see what was the cause of the delay. And he had stared into the ugliest face he had ever seen.

Angered at what he saw, he snarled, "Come on, hurry up, give me my change. Don't stare at me like that!"

Only then did he realize that the booth was empty, and the face he was looking at was his own reflection.

Big Bill's whole body sagged. He didn't feel so "big" anymore. He stepped out of the restroom and slumped down the aisle, bumping people as he went.

He collapsed into his seat, and squeezing his eyes shut, tried to sleep.

A jolt awakened him. The plane had landed.

Bill retrieved his bag from overhead and waited, head down, for the passengers ahead of him to get off the plane.

Coming out of the gate, Bill saw Doreen straight ahead of him, waiting with outstretched arms. Her eyes were bright and she had the broadest grin he'd ever seen.

"Dad!" she cried, and she ran forward to embrace him. "Dad! I'm so glad to see you! Oh I *love* you, Dad!"

Bill said, "Why do you like an old wretch like me?"

Doreen hugged him and said, "You're my *father*, Dad! I like you just the way you are."

Bill winced.

For Discussion

1. What is Bill's basic problem? See James 1:8; 4:8.

2. Does he recognize his plight?

3. Do you see yourself in him in any way?

4. Why does Doreen relate to him the way she does? Is she blind?

5. Do you see any comparisons between the daughter's attitude toward her father and God's relationship with us?

6. What is meant by "unconditional love"? See Romans 5:8.

On My Own Again

Sheri walked slowly up the outside stairway to the psychiatrist's office. She didn't really want to be here, and yet she did. She had to sort it all out.

She opened the outside door and found herself in a small waiting room. A buzzer sounded, and the psychiatrist, evidently alone in the office, greeted her briefly with a smile and said: "Hello. Would you please fill this card out? I'll be with you in a few moments."

Sheri acknowledged his greeting, sat down, and began to fill out the card. Name, address, health insurance—that was about it.

She settled back in her chair. She didn't really feel threatened, but it was a new experience. She hadn't been in a psychiatrist's office before, but a number of them had addressed her classes when she had gotten her M.A. in guidance and counseling 30 years ago.

So here she was. Fifty-five years old. Sheri Palmer. High school counselor. Mature woman. Good income. Respected in her field. And *divorced*.

All the bitterness of the last year assailed her again. Two years before, her life had been idyllic. Although she had accepted her single life after many years, she had finally capitulated when a handsome widower, a physician, had pressed her to marry him. Their marriage lasted one year. Then it happened—the old story—he began seeing a younger woman on the side. Their marriage collapsed, divorce followed, and here she was, bitter, distraught, unsure of herself.

Get some help, her friends said. Sort it all out. And now she sat here; a counselor waiting to be counseled.

The door opened and the psychiatrist ushered her into his office.

"I'm Dr. Brown," he said pleasantly, motioning her to a chair. The office was modestly furnished—a desk, some books. Two comfortable leather chairs faced each other by the window. There was a clock clearly visible on his desk.

Sheri laughed as she eased herself into a chair and noticed a box of Kleenex at her right elbow.

"All ready, I see," she smiled.

"Oh, yes, we use a lot of that around here," he smiled in response. "How can I help you?" he said directly.

Sheri began her account of what had brought her to the doctor's office. It came out slowly at first, but then the whole tale flowed freely. It actually felt good to get it out in the open—and with a trained person listening.

The psychiatrist said little. He offered mostly factual questions, or asked for clarifications.

Suddenly the hour was up. Sheri was a little surprised when he asked to see her again in a week. But then she remembered a friend had said: "The doctor doesn't really know you … it all takes time." And the psychiatrist himself closed the session by saying: "Remember, it's like an accordion. There's more at first, then fewer visits later."

And so the sessions continued. Once a week Sheri would climb the stairs, enter the office, push the Kleenex box aside with her elbow, and converse with the psychiatrist. Actually he spoke rarely—she was left to do most of the talking.

At one point religion came up. Sheri herself had been an active Christian years ago, but hadn't been to church for some time. She thought a friend had said Dr. Brown was a Christian and so she asked him about it.

"No," he responded. "I'm not hostile to Christianity. I believe in a God. But the main thing is that you have *faith*— Christian, Jewish, Buddhist—whatever. Don't you agree?"

Sheri didn't give him a straight yes on that one. In fact, she was surprised he had been that open with her about his convictions. She was a trained counselor herself. Your own point of view should be kept out of objective counseling.

But he had pursued the point momentarily. "I'm divorced from my wife, too ... I have three grown daughters. And all I want for them is to be *happy*. Isn't that all that's important in life?"

Again Sheri had not responded affirmatively, but just moved her head to indicate she was listening. But maybe that's when it all began. This man's philosophy of life was not her own. Well, what *was* her philosophy of life? She loved her work. Had dear friends. Was financially secure. But all toward what ultimate end? The question continued to disturb her as the sessions went on—one a week, for seven weeks.

Occasionally, when Sheri was not speaking, the psychiatrist would quietly ask, "What are you thinking about right now?"

But usually he didn't ask the question. And that's what particularly got to her—the *silences*. As a counselor Sheri knew the need to be an active listener and to say nothing at the right time. And here she was on the other end of the stick. And it was quite uncomfortable.

A minute would go by. Sheri would hear the roaring buses outside, look toward the window, and steal a glance at the clock. *Twenty minutes to go!* Yet, she told herself, as a trained professional she could handle the silence. And as the meetings went on, she got herself more under control. She felt she was in charge of her life again, and actually didn't need the psychiatrist any more. Indeed, he had confided to her that people who saw him generally fell into one of three categories: an anxiety reaction, depression, or a psychotic state. Sheri was in the first category and her anxiety was relatively mild, he said.

And so, as Sheri drove to her last session, she really felt it would be a waste of time. The religious discussion they had had continued to bother her. In fact, she had been doing some reading in recent weeks, books she still had from when she was attending church—C. S. Lewis, Dietrich Bonhoeffer, etc.—and those works really began to impress her again. And now a quote of Fulton Sheen, the Catholic cardinal on television many years ago, came to mind: "Psychology is good when used as an approach to theology, but the great theological truths are not psychological.... In theology we do not seek the identity of self. 'I live,' said the apostle Paul. (But) then he quickly checked himself 'No! Not I. Christ lives in me.' I am not my own. I am His."

Funny. As a Christian she believed that. She was not against psychology or psychiatry. Wherever one found truth—*real* truth—it was God's truth. It was God's gift to humanity. The skills and insights she had as a counselor were blessings from God.

Why hadn't she been giving God the credit for all the *good* things in her life?

Sheri found herself at the doctor's office and went in. The final meeting seemed rather innocuous to her. It was not really so much a counseling session as a conversation between two professionals. She felt he was no longer the doctor and she was his patient. For a moment she felt he hadn't helped her at all. Or maybe he had. In retrospect she realized the value of the sessions. Psychiatrists themselves went through psychoanalysis. And she would do this again, if it were ever necessary.

But for now, a deeper truth had emerged for her. She recalled a philosopher's statement that you can leave your home and go out for a long walk and come back and whom do you see sitting on the doorstep but—your *self*.

All this coursed through Sheri's mind as she slowly walked down the staircase after the last session.

She released a deep sigh. On the sidewalk ahead she noticed a white-uniformed nurse walking by. She was a dead ringer for Helen Patrick, a dear nurse friend from 20 years ago. She remembered visiting her in the hospital when Helen had contracted a long-term disease. Like herself, Helen was a Christian but had wandered away from the church.

Helen had said: "I've been far away from God in recent years. And this sickness has really brought me up sharply to ask myself *who* I am and *whose* I am and *where* I am going. Lying on this bed for six months has really brought me back closer to God. Thank God for it!"

A bus roared by. Sheri was brought sharply back to the present. The last meeting with the psychiatrist was over. She was on her own again. She would have to counsel her *self*. "Her own *self* sat on the doorstep in front of her."

Or would she? She remembered that very morning reading Dietrich Bonhoeffer's *Life Together*. And there was that one memorable statement after all the dialog: "And now I leave you to Christ and His Word."

Christ ... and His Word. She was not alone after all, Christ was with her, indeed, inside her through her Baptism, as old Pastor Schulze had taught her. It is "Christ in me." That's the way the apostle Paul put it.

Sheri looked up. The sky greeted her. There was no panic in heaven. She got into her car and headed for the high school.

For Discussion

1. What to you see as Sheri's *key* difficulty?

2. Should she have gone to a psychiatrist?

3. What do you think of the psychiatrist?

4. Do you think Sheri's problem is resolved?

5. Was her dilemma overcome too simplistically?

6. What do you feel the psychiatrist's feelings would be about Sheri's conclusions?

7. Certified, fully trained Christian psychiatrists are available throughout the country. But aren't there times a Christian should wish to see a secular psychiatrist to get a more "objective" point of view?

8. Study these Scripture references. Are such passages applicable in any way in this situation? Ephesians 4:14; 1 Timothy 6:3–5; 2 Timothy 3:13; 4:3–4; 2 Peter 2:1.

9. What should be Sheri's next step?

SESSION 5
Reaching Out

Let the People Say AMEN!

"Harry the Hippie," his friends had called him back in Clinton, Iowa. That's when he finally decided to leave his hometown and head out to "where the action was."

Berkeley. Of course. He'd hitch-hiked to the Bay Area. Seen *The City* first. Baghdad by the Bay. Then gone over to Berkeley.

And slept in People's Park at night and gotten a free meal every afternoon at a Lutheran church on College Avenue a block away.

1971. It was a good year.

For booze, and broads, and beer in the basement of a restaurant on Durant Avenue. Bought with nickels and dimes he had panhandled on Telegraph Avenue, pretending he was a representative of the "Free Clinic," with his little white tin box and come-on plea.

But then everything soured. Berkeley had changed. The riots were over. Students at the university were reading books again. And Telegraph Avenue had settled down to a bunch of middle-aged ex-Hippies trying to make a buck on leather belts and cheap jewelry.

So he hit the road again.

Vegas. Denver. Houston. Birmingham. Florida.

Yea, man! That's where they said to go. "Where the boys are." Broads, too, he'd heard.

But suddenly it was Christmas Day. A clear day. Not like many Christmas Days in Iowa. For sure, man.

The sun was usually bright here in Florida. And it was ... *Christmas Day*!

He remembered the small church he'd gone to in his youth.

The rustling of the sacks after the Christmas Eve service as the elders passed them to every child.

Some started eating the oranges at once, and he could still smell the tart, pungent odor of the split rinds.

Another place. Another time.

But this was Florida. And Christmas Day.

He should go to church.

And so he did.

It was a neat little church beside the bay. Boats bobbed in the harbor. Just as the toy boats his mother had bought him at Kress's years before—for him to play with in the bathtub when he took his Saturday evening bath. Bob. Bob. Bob.

On the boats he could hear the raucous sounds of men and women who'd started with an early morning Bloody Mary and hadn't let up since.

Christmas Day!

He was elated.

He was going to church again!

He walked in. Only a few people were visible. "A Blessed Christmas, sir," said a man with suit and tie, obviously an usher.

Harry bowed ever so slightly. The acid was beginning to get to him.

"Merry Christmas, shirr," he said. "Is there church today?"

"Of course—in about one-half hour."

Harry bowed again and walked elegantly through the doors of the foyer into the main part of the church.

Up by the altar, a minister had on a gown of some kind. On the back of it in large green letters were the words WONDER BREAD.

Awesome, man, awesome!

It was so neat to be in a church again.

Harry positioned himself in the dead center of the pews

and relaxed. He took the rubber band out of his ponytail, took the red bandanna from his forehead, and shook his hair loose.

He lit up a cigarette.

"Sorry, sir, we're very happy to have you here, but we don't smoke in church."

"Oh," said Harry, startled. "Of course."

With great dignity he stumbled out of the pew, into the aisle and back into the foyer again.

He was a nice guy, Harry thought. Very nice.

The acid hit him again.

Now he was in the back pew, conscious of his other "Harry" telling him to keep his act together. People began to arrive and soon the service began. There was an ellipsis of time for Harry ....

The preacher was delivering his sermon now. But Harry could see some broad water-skiing in her bikini on the water right outside the church windows.

The whole right side of the church was open windows, facing the bay. And everyone in the now-packed church could look out and see everything on the bay.

And there she was—a stunning young blonde chick with hair waving like a surrendering flag—in a bikini— going on her water skis back and forth outside the church's windows.

As the pastor tried to continue his sermon, Harry noticed each man in the congregation watched the blonde beauty fly by, their heads jerking to the right and left like spectators at a tennis game.

The women in the congregation, on the other hand, either watched the pastor with a frown and kicked their husband's leg, or gazed glazed-eyedly at the preacher. Fifty percent of them were secretly in love with him.

Next to Harry sat a young mother with a baby. The woman was cool and detached as she rocked her baby back and forth. Its little feet kept kicking Harry's leg. He loved it.

The mother had clean, black shiny hair. Her soft silk red blouse covered her olive skin. She had a sweet scent of musk and cinnamon about her. She smiled at Harry. She's just taken a shower, he thought.

The preacher was talking. Harry listened.

"Well, this was the week that was—for me," said the preacher.

"Little two-and-a-half-year old Kimberley Ann had an operation Monday. It was a very delicate operation to remove a tumor on her optic nerve.

"There were prayer warriors in this congregation, all over Florida, all over the nation, praying for that little girl this week.

"The doctor said he'd never felt such a force of prayer around him in that operating room. The operation took seven hours. The surgery went perfectly, he said.

"Kimberley Ann had a quick recovery. Saturday—yesterday afternoon—she was riding her tricycle on the driveway at her home!"

The preacher paused dramatically.

"What an awesome God we have! LET THE PEOPLE SAY AMEN!"

"AMEN!" the congregation responded in unison.

Harry had to hit the john.

He stumbled out of the pew and into the aisle.

His job done, he walked out the foyer of the little church and into the bright sunshine.

Christmas Day. Florida.

The boats were still tippling gently back and forth in the wind, like drunken sailors. The bikini girl was gone.

He could hear the congregation singing "Hark the Herald Angels Sing" in the background.

Christmas Day in Florida.

The tiny harbor glowed in the mid-day sun.

That broad in the bikini!

Not like that first stable scene, man!

Awesome, man, awesome!

Let the people say Amen!

AMEN!

For Discussion

Sort of a weird story, isn't it? But things like this *really happen*. Take, for instance, the time at a church in Concord, California, where a group of 50 Hell's Angels roared up into the parking lot just before the service was to begin. One Hell's Angel got off his bike, walked into the church, and sat down. The whole congregation watched fearfully, wondering what would happen next. But the rest of the bikers just stood in the parking lot and smoked their cigarettes during the hour, waiting for the service to end.

When it was over, some members talked to the bikers and invited the group to stay for coffee, which they did. Then they learned why the one biker had come to the service. He in some way had broken their "code," and as a punishment had to go to church.

Now perhaps going to church *is* a "punishment" for some people. And even for faithful Christians, at times it may be a "painful" experience, if the service is poorly planned or the sermon isn't too inspiring that day. More than once we may wince when we sing the lines in the hymn:

Grant us courage
For the facing of this hour.

1. But the real question is, if the Hell's Angels had appeared in *your* church parking lot, what would you and your fellow parishioners have done?

2. How "open" are we to people who are "different" from us?

An "Exclusive" Church

At a voter's meeting at a suburban church in St. Louis, one man moved that membership be "by invitation only."

At another church, a man whose neighbors' names had been turned in for a pastoral visit told his pastor: "Quite confidentially, Pastor, I don't think you would want them as members of our church. They just are not our kind of people."

A young woman visited another church. Barely 19, she had been a prostitute, had an illegitimate child, been married and divorced, and was on the way to alcoholism. But she wanted the help of the Gospel.

She had a beautiful voice, and the pastor suggested she join the church choir. She did, but after the first service in which she sang in the choir, the pastor heard an older member say to a friend: "And there she sat, right in the choir, along with the rest of us, just like she belonged there!"

In *Out of the Saltshaker and into the World* (Downers Grove, IL: Intervarsity Press, 1979), Rebecca Manley Pippert tells of a well-dressed middle-class congregation in Portland, Oregon, which wanted to reach out to the university students nearby. On one Sunday morning the church was crowded and there were no seats left. In walked a barefoot young man with mussed up hair, wearing blue jeans and a tee shirt.

People looked at him uncomfortably. He walked down the aisle, looking for a seat. When he got to the front pew and realized there were no seats, he just squatted on the carpet. She says, "The tension in the air became so thick one could slice it."

"Suddenly an elderly man began walking down the aisle toward the boy." What was he going to say to the young man? "The church became silent, all eyes were focused on him, you could hear anyone breathe. When the man reached (the boy), with some difficulty he lowered himself and sat down next to him on the carpet. I was told there was not a dry eye in the congregation" (p. 178).

For Discussion

1. Do you believe in the membership growth principle of homogeneity—that people should be directed to congregations of their own similar socioeconomic level, and parishes should gear their evangelization programs accordingly?

2. What do you feel attracts people to your church?

3. What are the first factors that might lead to the disenchantment of visitors to your church?

4. List the "inreach" and "outreach" programs of your congregation in parallel columns and evaluate them. What is your congregation's ministry to physically challenged (*formerly* called handicapped or disabled persons), blind or deaf persons, etc? What is your outreach to chemically dependent people?

5. Many evangelists hold that evangelization best occurs in "the living rooms and kitchens of the homes of the congregation. The most beautiful and natural place for the Gospel is ordinary folk in honest communication in their

homes talking and listening to one another about what really matters in life.... To become equal, to divest myself of any 'expert' status. I come not to get or want anything but to understand and to care." (Gerhard Knutson, *Listening Witness*, an outline of procedures for evangelism at St. James Lutheran Church, Crystal, Minnesota. I quoted Knutson in *The Compassionate Mind: Theological Dialog with the Educated* [St. Louis: Concordia Publishing House, 1990], pp. 185–86.) It is in such settings that genuine trust relationships can best be established. To what extent does that occur in your congregation?

6. Could you describe in detail to an inquirer what goes on in your pastor's adult instruction class (for those interested in joining your congregation)?

7. A small protestant church in Manteca, California, had a rundown church building, even using old theater seats for chairs. The pastor said, "We're too hifalutin for the fruit pickers. They go to the Pentecostal church on the edge of town. There, you don't have to wear shoes." What would you do as an usher if a shoeless, shirtless young man entered your church for services? See Exodus 22:21; Matthew 25:35; Hebrews 13:2, 3 John 5–6.

SESSION 6
Love and Aging

The Lover

It had been five years since his wife, Dell, died. Yet it seemed like yesterday.

And three years had passed since he had retired as sales manager for Bethlehem Steel.

So Lou Harkness had traveled. He'd spent months in most of the major cities of western Europe; but Strasbourg appealed to him the most.

Now he was sitting in *La Petite Bouffe* again, overlooking the scenic canal.

Geraniums trailed down in profuse colors from the flower boxes outside the 16th-century-styled windows. A tourist boat floated by, headed for the locks. He heard the faint sound of an accordion in the distance.

Lou felt the pleasant familiarity of the place envelop him. He was at peace. And yet a quiet excitement began to stir in him.

He was waiting for her.

The waiter, speaking in French with a faint Alsatian accent, asked Lou if he wished for a glass of wine before dining.

"*Sprechen sie Deutsch?*" Lou countered, knowing most adult Strasbourgers also spoke German, since the city had been German until 1918.

"*Natürlich,*" said the waiter, somewhat condescendingly.

"Weisswein, bitte."

The waiter bowed, and Lou saw a trio of bright young students, probably from the *Université*, take the table next to him.

"Ah, flaming youth," he joked to himself. Immediately his mind turned to his own carefree teenage years.

And Mary Jane.

She was blonde and beautiful. Both 17. He had fallen "head over heels" in love with her.

Now he called it infatuation. He was so young, so immature, so naive! But it was the first time he had been touched by love in that way.

He remembered his first kiss (beside that of his mother's whenever she tucked him into bed). It happened out in the garage behind the old farmhouse near Clinton, Iowa. It was Judy, the girl from the next farm. They had sat on the running board of the Ford, and embraced. They were only 10 years old. And they kissed.

Then in boarding school he passed notes to a girl from Arkansas. His mother found one in the laundry that he sent home each week. When his mother read, "Well, let nature take its course," she thought the girl was pregnant, but all he'd meant was that they would allow their friendship to grow. His mother and her imagination! Wild! They were only 14 years old! And that was in 1939!

"The Great Lover" at that age? But he went to all of the Nelson Eddy and Jeannette MacDonald movies, and came home to sing the songs to himself in front of the mirror. He'd arch his eyebrows and lift his head high at the final note. He sometimes asked his mother if she believed he was good-looking. She'd always say, "Lou, my boy, you will always be good-looking to me."

But that was not what he wanted to hear.

He met Mary Jane when he was 17, and wondered if *she* thought he was handsome. He often watched her from his dorm window at the small Iowa Bible college they attended.

She had dancing eyes and an engaging smile. Yet she could be so elusive. And when she walked her slim hips wiggled and bounced from side to side.

Though he wanted to ask her out for some hot chocolate at Albert's Place, the campus gathering spot, he was afraid to.

And then one day, through a mutual friend, "Middleman Suzie" they called her, he was able to send a message to Mary Jane, informing her he would like to date her.

They had met at her dorm, and walked to Albert's Place. As they enjoyed hot chocolate, they talked about the latest Glenn Miller records. He had been so nervous he scalded his tongue as he drank the hot chocolate, and it had hurt for three days.

They had a few more dates, and then one night, just as the dorm was closing at 9:30 p.m., he remembered, he asked if he could kiss her good night. And she had said yes.

So he had kissed her. It was a sweet and gentle kiss, the first since Judy had kissed him when he was 10.

He remembered it so clearly. He said good-night and walked away. It was literally like *walking on air*. He scarcely felt the sidewalk under his feet. Elated, he felt like he was walking on the moon.

In time, Mary Jane lost interest in him—went with some basketball player at the nearby Presbyterian college. Some called her "The Blonde Bomber." He heard she and the captain of the team "necked" on the hill behind the gymnasium.

He was crushed. Defeated. His first love. But he would always remember her and their first kiss.

The waiter brought Lou's wine, and Lou thanked him. It was cool, smooth, relaxing. And so was the setting sun around him.

Amanda was late. No matter. She could twist him around her little finger. He didn't mind waiting.

He let his mind wander into the past.

Outside the window, another tourist boat went by. He waved to a number of school children crowded in the fantail of the boat. He heard the deep-throated tolling of the bell at the Strasbourg Cathedral in the distance. How vividly he remembered attending mass there with Dell.

Dell! His beloved wife of so many years. What a fantastic woman!

Naturally there had been other "loves" before her.

His first love—Mary Jane. Or rather, first infatuation.

Then there had been Robin. How he was taken in by her. She fantasized to everyone about what a wealthy life she had lived back home, which some of the students later learned never existed. She was a gifted flautist, but incredibly self-centered. How he had fallen for her! And he remembered the last date, when he quietly said he wouldn't be seeing her again. She couldn't believe it. But he stuck to his word.

There had been Betsy, trusting, tender, self-giving, utterly open and honest. They carved their initials on the "stacks" in the library and talked of a future together. But she was older than he was, and he was afraid of any long-term commitment at that point. He had not been fair to her. He had hurt her. Long ago he had asked her—and God—to forgive him.

"What might have been," Lou thought.

The three coeds at the next table were into their *torte flambe* now, and Lou basked in their bright, happy conversation. Ah, they have all of their lives—and their loves—ahead of them, he thought.

He looked at the small brown spots on his hands. His mother had had a good many as she aged. Now you're aging, friend, he told himself.

But Amanda was coming!

He glanced at his watch again. Dell had given it to him.

She had been solid, secure, self-sacrificing. A person of deep trust and loyalty. It had been a good marriage. A gift from God. He had loved her deeply. And still did. But she was gone and life went on. It had to.

Their three sons had brought great joy into their home. All were married now, with grown children of their own, all off to different universities. How time had flown. How he had loved playing with those boys over the years in their backyard.

He had retired two years after Dell's death. As he traveled, he had reflected, and so many things came into perspective.

He looked back. *What different kinds of love God had given him!* What unusual gifts God gives us in so many different ways.

And now he had found a new love. It was a refined

love—a more mature kind of love. He had thought he would always be lonely after Dell had gone. But God had given him a new outlet for his affection.

And he was to see her again. Very soon.

At that moment Amanda walked through the door. She was entrancing. She flashed a smile at him as she strode across the room to his table by the window. What grace!

He seated her opposite him and then looked long and lovingly into her clear blue eyes.

"I love you, Amanda," Lou said. "And I want you to know I'll do anything I can to make you happy."

"Yes, Grandpa, I know," Amanda replied.

For Discussion

1. What struck you most about this story?

2. What insights did you gain from Lou Harkness's reminiscences?

3. As life changes, and we (hopefully) mature, our perceptions shift. The "loves" of the past are seen from a distance. We recall different "loves." The greatest incarnation of love is God Himself. Study these Scripture passages and compare them to the common, often superficial, uses of the word *love*. God's love: John 3:16; Romans 5:7, 8; Ephesians 2:4–5; 1 John 3:1. Our love toward God: Deuteronomy 6:5;

2 Thessalonians 3:5; Jude 21. Love toward others: Matthew 22:39; John 13:34, 35; 15:12; 1 Peter 1:22. And note that the great "Love Chapter," 1 Corinthians 13, really begins with 1 Corinthians 12:31b.

4. An "in" word these days is *bonding*. A mother "bonds" with her child, a father with his son, spending "quality" time in deepening and enriching their relationship. In some areas, even in Christian congregations, a man or woman may "bond" with a person of the opposite gender who is not their spouse. It is understood that the relationship is purely platonic (intellectual and social) without *any* romantic involvement. There is simply a deep, common sharing of mutual interests and the nurture of a fine Christian friendship. What do you think of this trend?

The Romantic

Greying Art Wright, retired architect, sat in the deep leather easy chair in his den. He was going through old files, discarding some, marking others for his protege, Jim Mason.

He leaned back and sighed. Straight ahead of him, among dozens of other pictures on the wall, was the stunning photo of his wife, Julia, taken on their honeymoon at Vail. She was 22 then. He stared at her singular beauty. She had long, dark hair, and she presented a striking figure in her svelte ski outfit. There she stood, arms akimbo, confidently grinning at him with her irresistible smile. What a girl!

Art shook his head and went on with his work. He picked up an old file marked "PERSONAL." He hadn't looked at this packet of stuff in ages. Opening the sheaf of papers he noticed a handwritten letter: December 10, 1939. It began: "To My Future Wife. Darling ..."

Art frowned, gave a little laugh, pushed the other papers aside, and began reading. Then he paused momentarily, fixing the date in his mind. December 10, 1939. He was still single then, a student at Washington University in St. Louis. He had one more year to go before heading for architectural school. He remembered those lonely years all too well. He began again:

To My Future Wife

Darling—

Sitting here at my drawing board I am stirred to sentimentality by the soul-inspiring music of Mendelssohn's *Italian Symphony* on my phonograph. I just happened to think of writing to my wife—the woman God will send to me whom I do not yet know. I smile in expectancy.

I miss you so much in my daily life. I dream of all the little things we could say to each other. I think of the things I could do for you, the plans we could make, what we could do for other people.... And all this with the knowledge that when our life is over on earth we'll still see each other in heaven....

I feel inadequate about the times I haven't best prepared myself for the husband I want you to have....

When I was younger, getting married seemed like such a "bind" to me. But now, when I think of you, I realize how beautiful it can be. Husband and wife! Blessed with God's love and care! What greater joy is there in life?

I dream about you often. Not only about "a girl" or "my wife" but about YOU, and no one else in the world. I feel there's only one person in the world for me, that we're waiting for each other, and that our meeting lies in God's hands.

There's only one YOU, and I'm waiting for you, dearest.

61

Art groaned and then guffawed. What a romanticist I was! And that was almost 60 years ago! Then he cracked up. Tears came to his eyes, and wiping them away with his hand he read on.

Sometimes I wonder exactly how I will propose to you.... But another thought disturbs me more. I'm still in a quandary about just where my niche is in God's universe—professionally, I mean. Architecture woos me, but I'd like to write symphonies, in fact, be a symphony conductor. I want to travel, I want to write, I want to ski on the highest mountain peaks in Switzerland. I want a family and real "children of God" to do His work....

No, what I really want most is to give you my love. And that's what worries me. I love you so much. And yet, knowing my shortcomings, and wanting you to have only the very best, I ... well, I pray you will be able to accept me, as I believe Christ has accepted me....

These are thrilling days I'm living in—and for this reason: every time I go to church, or to a program, or a party, I always feel that "here is where I might meet my wife."

Funny, isn't it? But for me, it's very real and very true. Just think! "I'm going to meet you tonight for the first time!" That's what goes through my mind every time.

And then one day I'll look back and say: "I met her the time when...."

Tonight I attend the St. Louis Symphony concert in Kiel Auditorium. As I take the streetcar downtown I'll see all the Christmas lights along the way. The true spirit of Christmas is in my heart right now, for Christ is there, I am thinking of you, and I am very happy!

I wonder when we'll read this?—on our honeymoon? I WISH WE WERE THERE!

I've probably seen a thousand too many movies, but I sure love to reminisce into the future about you ... how we'll meet ... when I'll first know YOU are the one I'm writing this to....

Remind me to kiss you just for old times' sake (THESE times).

God be with you till we meet ... THEN.

I love you,

Art

P.S. 6:45–7:45 p.m. What are you doing?

Art sighed again and leaned way back in his chair. Well, God *had* answered his prayers. For while at home that Christmas in 1939 he had met Julia at a party. It was the closest thing to love at first sight one could imagine. They had danced together and he would never, *never* forget how their eyes had locked on each others' throughout the evening.

Her beauty had sent him reeling. And all through his life he remembered her from those first days. She was to be eternally young in his eyes. But it wasn't only her physical beauty that Art admired. It was really the inner Julia—for she strongly shared the Christian faith in which they were married.

And those early memories of Julia stayed with Art in the years that followed: their honeymoon at Vail, their struggling years while he finished architectural school, then his first job in Denver, and finally his very successful 40-year career as the leading architect in burgeoning Phoenix.

Julia. God's lovely gift to him.

Art got up and walked into the kitchen. Standing by the stove he saw an enchanting young woman stirring a sauce pan. Her hair was long and dark. Her opaline eyes smiled at him, and her lips parted in a teasing grin.

Julia Wright stirred the sauce. It was hard to do now as she leaned on her walker. Bald spots shone through her thin, white hair. Little flecks of brown showed on her wrinkled, arthritic hands. Blurred eyes peered through thick glasses, which looked like the bottoms of coke bottles.

Art grabbed Julia, pulled her to him, and kissed her soundly.

"Julia, you're beautiful!" he said.

Julia almost fell out of her walker.

"Art, you're an old fool," she laughed.

For Discussion

1. Is Art Wright an "old fool"?

2. Is "love at first sight" possible? Is it wise?

3. "Beauty is only skin deep." What do you think is the real basis of Art and Julia's relationship?

4. Do we ever live with false idealizations of the opposite sex?

5. Is the idea of "one person in the world for me" realistic? Is it self-serving?

6. Does God have a "plan" for our lives? How does the Christian find out what "God's plan" may be? A young seminary student said this: "If the good Lord wants me to get married, he knows my address: Concordia Seminary, St. Louis, Missouri." How does the Christian know the difference between "waiting on the Lord" (Psalm 27) and taking action on one's own?

7. What are the clues to "a love that never ends"? See 1 Corinthians 12:31; 13:13; Ephesians 5:22–29; Colossians 3:19; 1 Peter 3:1.

8. Does this story have any relevance for divorced people? For persons who are single?

HELPS FOR THE LEADER
Introduction

Please read "About This Book" at the beginning of this Study Guide. It is noted there that these short story Bible studies can be utilized in several ways:

☐ In small home-discussion groups
☐ In the Sunday morning Bible class
☐ In a weekday Bible class at church
☐ In individual reading and meditation for spiritual nourishment

There are 4, 6-session courses in this series. Each session is based on one or more short stories, arranged topically according to thematic issues, with discussion questions referencing Bible texts designed to lead the learner to apply Scripture to his/her own life.

Because the story/stories for each session can be read in an average of 9 minutes (range, 5–13 minutes), the stories could be read at the time of meeting—either silently by each participant before discussion or aloud by selected readers in the group. A third alternative is that the stories be read beforehand.

Setting Up the Course

Whatever setting for a group is chosen, a key element in publicity is *This is a different kind of Bible study!* For example:

Jesus told stories. And we are also going to deal with real-life stories from our world. In them we may see ourselves, seek to better understand ourselves, and see how we as Christians relate to other people. But our ultimate objective is reading "short stories leading into the Word." There, in "searching the Scriptures" we really determine who we are and whose we are and where we are going.

Beginning the Class

Size of the Group

Depending on how many people sign up to attend the course, decide how many separate groups you should have!

Remember, *the magic number is 10* (give or take 1 or 2). In groups larger than 10, many individuals don't have a chance to contribute. In too small a group some persons may feel intimidated and "freeze," especially on sensitive issues. If your class size is greater than 10 and you have only one leader, consider breaking into groups of four for small-group discussion of the questions (30 minutes). Then use the rest of the session for sharing with the total group the discoveries and the "help us with the answer to number___" questions of the small groups.

So decide well in advance how many groups—and *prepared* group leaders—you should have.

The Setting

Be sure the group meets in as comfortable a setting as possible. Are participants more at ease around a table? Check the thermostat. Make sure the lighting is good.

Have refreshments arranged well ahead of time.

Provide extra Bibles and hymnals for those who didn't bring their own.

Presession

As group leader, be sure you arrive *before anyone else does.*

Welcome the arrivals. Introduce people who don't know each other. Don't presume they all do.

As participants are seated, be sure they can all see each other.

Opening the Session

Begin with a brief prayer. Ask for the blessing of the Holy Spirit.

Then comment on the procedure:

- The story (stories) will be read (silently, or by a *good*, carefully selected reader).
- The discussion questions will follow.
- No one will be *pressed* to answer questions. No one will be embarrassed or put on the spot.
- Turn to the *four key questions* in this guide and note how these are to be kept in mind in dealing with each story throughout the course:

  1. Is the story true to life? Give reasons for your answer.

  2. What, if anything, does the story have to say to our Christian faith and life?

  3. How does it reveal or point to our need? (Law)

  4. How does it point to or suggest God's action for us in Christ? (Gospel)

If some finish reading the story/stories before others, request that they reflect on the four questions until the others are done.

Note. In many groups, processing these four questions will consume *all* the time in a 50-minute session. Also, the questions after the story will probably take more than the time available. Therefore, decide on one of two strategies: *Either* agree to stick to the 1-hour or 1½ hour regular session time for each session, selecting among the questions only those that can be handled during the time available, *or* move through the stories and questions according to the interests of the group, leaving open-ended the amount of time it will take to complete the course.

The Art of Asking Questions

And now to some general considerations about leading the discussion after the stories are read:

"Telling is not teaching." Learning does not occur as much when a discussion leader does most of the talking.

A good leader, therefore, utilizes the art of *inductive* questioning—"drawing people out."

Good questions facilitate INTERACTION,
- which yields INNER ACTION,
- which precedes LEARNING.

Good questions MOTIVATE learners to
- THINK and
- EXPRESS themselves and become more
- INVOLVED in the process of their own
- LEARNING.

What kinds of questions should you put to your group? *How to Teach Adults* (St. Louis: CPH, 1992) recommends questions that are

- **brief**—in as few words as possible.
- **open**—encouraging participants to think for themselves.
- **specific**—identified with words or ideas in your class study guide or used in your class conversations.
- **clean**—easily understood.
- **focused**—involving only one point.
- **purposeful**—stimulating the participant to
  —recall a fact or event;
  —analyze concepts and ideas and their relationships in order to discover meaning in them;
  —evaluate meanings to determine whether the participants agree or disagree with them and decide for or against them.
- **concrete**—calling for definite examples.

Don't answer your own questions. Wait for an answer—even though the waiting period can seem interminable.

Avoid these types of questions:

- How could you even think about voting for such a liberal candidate? (Too harassing.)
- Tell us about the creation of the world. (Too vague.)
- Why must we support a candidate with views like hers? (Too leading.)
- What about a historical Adam and Eve? (Well, what about them?)
- Did Adam and Eve know what would result from their disobedience? (Too simple. Yes or No.)
- Did God create life anywhere other than on earth? (Too much speculation.)
- Come on now, you surely know the name of the first murderer, don't you? (Too condescending.)

For practice in formulating and evaluating questions, evaluate the discussion questions in this book or in other adult-education materials. What good questions do you see? Why are they good or appropriate or helpful? How could they be improved?

Undoubtedly, members of your group will raise some excellent questions. Be slow to answer them. Rather, bounce the questions back to the others in your group. That will help keep your discussions lively and interesting. Especially encourage people to use the words *why* and *how* as they begin their questions. Those questions lead to deeper thought and more precise application.

If you have one of the first two courses in this series—*The Perfect Couple* and *The Bright Red Sports Car*—see the introduction to the Leaders Guides for additional suggestions regarding the art of asking questions.

The Real Word for the Real World

A final point needs emphasis. Evangelical writer Elizabeth Elliott has said that "almost everything in the Bible is the reverse of what the world says." Certain group members, especially those addicted to some television shows, may have had their values shaped far more by the mass media than by the means of grace. As J. B. Phillips translates Romans 12:2:

> Don't let the world around you squeeze you into its own mould, but let God re-make you so that your whole attitude of mind is changed. Thus you will prove in practice that the will of God's good, acceptable to Him and perfect.

That kind of perspective comes only from our Lord Jesus Christ—cradled in the Scriptures. The Word interprets the world. It's not the other way around. Your task is to direct group members back to the values and priorities in God's Holy Word.

Toward that end, keep the four key questions of this series in mind.

1. Is the story true to life? Give reasons for your answer.

2. What, if anything, does the story have to say to our Christian faith and life?

3. How does it reveal or point to our need? (Law)

71

4. How does it point to or suggest God's action for us in Christ? (Gospel)

And may you be a prayerful, prepared, and compassionate discussion leader!

For additional help in your preparation, see *How to Teach Adults* (mentioned earlier) or "Developing Skills for Teaching Adults" from the *Teaching the Faith* video series (St. Louis: CPH, 1993).

SESSION 1
Forgiveness

Stories

The Unlocked Door
Freedom Vignettes

For Discussion

1. **"Freedom" is really a state of mind. Do you agree? See John 8:36; Romans 6:1–11; Galatians 2:20.** "You are freed indeed," says Jesus. Our freedom in Christ is based on the objective reality of what Christ has done for us—a reality that's "there" regardless of our attitude. But that reality—indeed, Christ Himself—reshapes our minds and affections so that we can *act* as free as He has made us to be.

2. **Freedom also involves an *awareness and acceptance* of our emancipation. (Not that we get "credit" for "choosing" God. He has chosen us. But our rejection of His gracious act of redemption nullifies its effect.) The parolee was no longer under condemnation, but didn't realize it. Similarly, our forgiveness and freedom in Christ took place a long time ago. How do these Scripture passages underscore that point? See Romans 8:28–30; Ephesians 1:4; 1 Peter 1:18–20; Hebrews 9:28.** Ask individual volunteers to read each text. Encourage comments on each.

3. **"So if the Son sets you free, you will be free indeed" John 8:36. As Christians, we are really like the freed eagle. Yet we often live as if various**

73

"chains" still bind and inhibit us. What *imagined* bonds do many people still need to free themselves from? See Romans 6:9; Matthew 10:29 ff; Hebrews 13:5b; Philippians 4:11; and 1 Peter 5:7.

The question is meant to be provocative. Here you may first want to explore the *actual* "chains" that try to bind us in our Christian lives: e.g., (a) the Old Person of sin still "kicking around" inside each of us; (b) all of Satan's attempts at enslavement—often in a new and different guise every day; (c) the subtle entrapments of the mass media and our pagan culture.

Then explore those *imagined* chains.

- We need not *fear death*, for Christ has conquered death. See Romans 6:9.
- We need not *fear for our welfare*. See Matthew 10:29ff.
- We need not be *lonely*. See Hebrews 13:5b.
- We need not *live in anxiety*. See Philippians 4:11.
- We are not to *doubt God's constant care* and love for us. See 1 Peter 5:7.

What other *imagined* chains can you deal with here?

4. Is there a "jail ministry" in your community? Is your congregation involved? What preventive measures against crime is your community involved in?

Here you may wish to explore the answers to these questions with information you gather *before* this class session. Also you may wish to have a person present who can answer these questions knowledgeably.

Prayer

Lord, teach me how to pray. Open. Expectant. *Believing!* Not trying to bend Your will to mine, but always open to Your grand design. And then *thankful*. For whatever answer You give. In the name of the almighty Father, and the strong name of His Son, Jesus Christ, and in the blessed name of the Holy Spirit. Amen.

Hymn

"We Praise You, O God"

Life with Others

Story

A Neatly Ordered Life

For Discussion

1. How do you evaluate the world-view of Bettye Langley?

Bettye Langley, of course, is a classic example of a person "curved in on oneself" (Luther). But one almost has to feel sorry for her. Or do you?

2. What can you say in her defense? Doesn't her approach to life and her relationship with other people seem totally logical to her?

Bettye may feel "secure" in her world-view. But how could a loving fellow Christian help her break free of what is really a self-made prison cell?

3. Do you see part of yourself in Bettye Langley? In what way? In what ways are your attitudes toward other people justified and in what ways do you think you should change? See 1 Corinthians 10:12.

All of us can be inclined to control or at least manipulate other people. 1 Corinthians 10:12 reminds us to "be careful that you don't fall." This is why daily self-examination is so important. See Luther's "Christian Questions with Their Answers." We also need to rediscover "A Blessing Often Overlooked"—Private Confession and Holy Absolution.

4. Anne Morrow Lindbergh said, "Him that I love

I wish to be *free*—even from me!" Why don't we truly free others? If we don't free them, doesn't that mean we don't really love them?

Touché! With the Old Person of sin still within us, we are inclined to love self more than God or others. "We have a way of committing the original sin all over again—every day." "You shall be as gods" Satan said in conning Eve and Adam (Gen. 3:5). May we be moved to pray: "Lord, forgive me for my self-love. By Your Holy Spirit empower me to love You with my whole heart, soul and mind—and my neighbor as myself."

5. (Study of 1 Corinthians. See Study Guide.)

6. Study Philippians 2:1–11. What particular message is there that speaks to the "selfish self" in each of us? How does the Gospel in the latter verses apply to all of this?

We are to "pour ourselves out" as Jesus did, by the power of the Holy Spirit alone, ridding ourselves of the "selfish self" within each of us. However, we do not "work on" humility and selflessness.

> Now we are not just speaking of "virtues to emulate." That would be the evil of moralism. Moralism holds up certain values as ideals to follow, rather than seeing them as consequences of the Gospel. We don't "work on" traits of Christian character. For Christ is not just "our example." He is rather our prototype. He is the firstfruits of those who believe in Him. Therefore we focus not on His humility, as a precept to follow, but on His humiliation—His sacrifice for us. For we fail totally. But through His death and resurrection we are forgiven and then called to the fruits of faith, empowered totally by the Holy Spirit. It is "Christ in me." Paul uses the phrase repeatedly in the New Testament....

> Moralism is demonic because it tells me to "shape up"—but as a sinner I know I cannot. Only the Gospel heartens me, for it tells me that I am forgiven for my failure and points to the cross of Christ. Christ does that in me which I cannot do.

> As noted in discussing the positive prescription of the Ten Commandments, it is not really the Christian "doing it" at all, but *Christ*, as Paul says:

> I live; yet not I, but Christ liveth in me: and the life which I

now live in the flesh I live by the faith of the Son of God, who loved me, and gave Himself for me. (Galatians 2:20)

(From "Great Dangers Facing the Teacher and Preacher," *Lutheran Education*, September/October, 1991, pp. 4–12. By the author.)

Story

A Glad Heart

For Discussion

1. How do you feel Amy is handling the new chapter in her life?

Answers will vary.

2. Do you think Amy's personality was a little "strange?" Why or why not?

How insensitive we can be to other people whose personalities are not like our own! Here the group may share—in a jovial way—what some of their own unique habits or eccentricities may be (or that of their spouses).

3. What does 1 Corinthians 12 have to say about differing personalities? Romans 12?

In the church all are joined to each other—in Christ. But in practice often our problem is that we are *not* joining in with each other.

A little girl on a farm was told by her father to always come back to the house before it got dark, especially when it was winter, and freezing cold outside. One time, however, during a severe freeze, the little girl had been playing alone in the cornfield, and did not return to the house.

The farmer searched and searched for his daughter, but to no avail. It was now below freezing, and the wind came up, with a deadly chill factor. Quickly he called his neighbors, and they joined in their search for the child. But again they could not find her.

Finally, in desperation, one man said, "Let's join hands and search the field systematically together." They did that, and finally found the child. But it was too late. She had frozen to death.

The father, grief-stricken, cried out, "MY GOD! Why weren't we holding hands together before!?"

Why haven't we been holding hands together ... before?

4. Does God really "call" a person to a single life? See 1 Timothy 5:14. Do Paul's words to Timothy mandate marriage? (See also 1 Corinthians 7:7ff.)

Of course, Paul is not mandating marriage here—as he did not of *himself*. See 1 Corinthians 7:8ff. Again, Christians have different gifts—and some live in the state of marriage and some do not. See 1 Corinthians 7:7.

5. What is the difference between loneliness and solitude? Are you a "solitude" person? How does one *avoid* loneliness but *find* solitude?

ON OVERCOMING LONELINESS

(1) "Be still and know that God is God" (Psalm 46). Set aside a definite time for Bible reading and prayer.

(2) Give thanks—for the promise of God's presence. He's still in charge—and is preparing "for us" an eternal weight of glory beyond all comparison.

(3) Refuse self-pity—a death that has no resurrection. Don't dwell on your own losses—or envy others. Christ bore and carried our sorrow—not that we might not suffer, but that our sufferings might be like His.

(4) Accept your loneliness. It can be a stage—a vocation— to realize our helplessness and be drawn closer to God.

(5) Offer up your loneliness to God…. Give it to Him as a gift and let Him transform it.

(6) Do something for somebody else. Take definite, overt action to overcome the inertia of grief. (See Isaiah 58:10–12). Pour yourself out.

(Adapted from Elizabeth Elliott, "The Ones Who Are Left," *Christianity Today*, Feb. 27, 1976, p. 7.)

God says: "I know your depression. I care for you." "I will never leave you, nor forsake you." (Hebrews 13:5)

Prayer

When I am down, Lord, empower me by Your Holy Spirit to look *up* to the hills of Your strength. Make me know and assure me that I am never alone—but that You are always by my side. Bless me with the daily consciousness of Your holy angels who minister to me—as they did to Your Son, my Savior. In the strong name of Jesus Christ. Amen.

Hymn

"Let Us Ever Walk with Jesus"

SESSION 3

Communication

Story

Don't You Like My Present?

For Discussion

1. What do you feel is the *real* source of Chris's loneliness?

Answers to this question may vary. Some may focus on Chris's apparent self-pity. Others may say Eunice is at fault, closing him out of a more intimate relationship. Don't try to draw final conclusions at this point but be ready to move to question 2.

2. What do you think of the comment, "I think Chris's solution to the problem is just a matter of 'putting up with a bad situation' "?

You might probe whether this comment is a description of what Chris *is* doing or what he *should* do. You might also ask whether the apostle Paul's words apply here: "I have learned to be content whatever the circumstances" (Philippians 4:11). Or see James 1:2–3 and discuss how one can be joyful and *welcome* testing (which produces perseverance).

3. At one point Chris wondered if he was "feeling too sorry for himself." Elizabeth Elliott has said "to hell with self-pity." Catherine Marshall speaks of how a degree of self-pity can join the blown-up pride of our self-congratulation at having been so patient and reliable with other people and calls the mixture a

"deadly brew" (*Something More, p. 137*). Author Hannah Smith said "All discouragement is of the devil." What does Scripture have to say about all this? See Genesis 50:20; Matthew 6:25, 32; 1 Peter 5:7; 2 Corinthians 12:9–10.

You might note that Chris is self-critical in admitting self-pity. It's a trap Satan sets for all of us. At the same time, he moves toward self-effacement and thankfulness to God for Eunice *as she is* near the end of the story. Let individuals read the texts and invite comments.

4. What can lead to the loss of intimacy in a marriage? In this story what do you think were the key factors?

Answers will vary.

5. The story spoke of "viewing one's spouse as a *present* from God." In what ways could that perspective change an otherwise humdrum or perfunctory relationship?

Again, we need to focus on the difference of gifts (1 Corinthians 12) and personalities with which God has endowed us. Examination can also be made of the *false* expectations of the opposite sex in marriage, which our pagan culture foists upon us ("stunning blonde," "tall, dark, and handsome," and all the youth-oriented imageries).

"A man is never old if he can still be moved emotionally by a woman of his own age." (James Michener, *The Source*, p. 431)

6. Whether you are single or married, what do you look for most in making a friend or seeking a life partner? See John 15:13; Romans 12:9–10. Also Ephesians 5:21, 22, 25; 1 Peter 3:1–2; 7–9.

Even secular studies reveal that the qualities people look for in a mate (or for singles, a good friend) are not first of all physical characteristics. Explore what these attributes are (trusting, caring, kindness, compassion, tolerance, understanding, etc.).

Prayer

Lord, please be merciful and forgive me for the times I have hurt my partner. By Your Holy Spirit enable both of us to forgive each other and to live selflessly for each other. Create a fresh bond of peace and mutual helpfulness between us that we may, by Your Holy Spirit's power, do Your will—both where we live now and wherever You call us to serve. In the strong name of Jesus Christ. Amen.

Hymn

"Lord Divine, All Love Excelling"

Self-Awareness

Story

The Ugliest Face He'd Ever Seen

For Discussion

1. What is Bill's basic problem? See James 1:8; 4:8.

Would to God that we could "see ourselves as others see us."

2. Does he recognize his plight?

Partially. He *does* call himself an "old wretch" and winces when he sees the authentic, loving acceptance of his daughter.

3. Do you see yourself in him in any way?

Be ready to move on to question 4. Some people may not want to open up on this question readily.

4. Why does Doreen relate to him the way she does? Is she blind?

Martin Luther once said that we are drawn to infants and toddlers because of their open, guileless trust in us. Their innocence reminds us of mankind's blessed state before the Fall. Doreen's love for her father was open, honest, and absolutely trusting.

5. Do you see any comparison between the daughter's attitude toward her father and God's relationship with us?

The question is so closely related to question 6 ("What is meant by 'unconditional love'?") you may want to discuss them simultaneously.

God accepts us "as we are." Whatever our age, race, color, or personality type, He says "I have redeemed you; I have summoned you by name; you are Mine" (Isaiah 43:1). "See, I have engraved you on the palms of My hands" (Isaiah 49:16).

He accepts us "unconditionally." He does not say "*if* you will do this, *then* I will accept you." He rather says "*because* my Son suffered and died for you on the cross; *therefore* be what you are—a redeemed, loved, accepted, and forgiven child of Mine."

He continues: "Do not take My forgiveness lightly. It is not 'cheap grace' but 'costly grace'—the suffering and death of My Son.

"I have accepted you, the unacceptable. I have loved you, the unlovable. Now! Do not 'sin more that grace may abound.' Rather, 'go and sin no more.' I hate your sin. But I love *you*, sinner that you are.

"I accept you ... *unconditionally.*"

Story

On My Own Again

For Discussion

1. What do you see as Sheri's *key* difficulty?

Answers may vary. Try to stay with the actual facts/statements in the story. Some people may recall their own visits to counselors. Don't press them to reveal details they may not wish to share, or which they may reveal and wish later they had *not*.

2. Should she have gone to a psychiatrist?

Here is an opportunity to stress the blessing God has given us in skilled counselors, and to dispel the stigma of going to a "shrink." There can also be fruitful discussion of the pastor's role as a spiritual counselor—and the "Blessing Often Overlooked"—the Sacrament of Private Confession and Holy Absolution. But a properly trained pastor (who is *not* a psychiatrist!) will also know the time to *refer* a person to a qualified psychiatrist.

3. What do you think of the psychiatrist?

Answers will vary.

4. Do you think Sheri's problem is resolved?

Only time will tell. The question is whether—by the power of the Holy Spirit—Sheri will act on her renewed insights and utilize the means of grace—the Word of God in the Scripture, Holy Baptism, the Eucharist, and Private Confession and Holy Absolution. Often our greatest problem is simply that *we don't use the means of grace!*

5. Was her dilemma overcome too simplistically?

Not necessarily. Often it's as simple as that. We are not really hooked up to the power supply of God's grace: Word and Sacrament.

6. What do you feel the psychiatrist's feelings would be about Sheri's conclusions?

This is only conjecture. You may want to note, though, that his amorphous, universalistic philosophy should have no impact on Sheri's own Christian faith.

7. Certified, fully trained Christian psychiatrists are available throughout the country. But aren't there times a Christian should wish to see a secular psychiatrist to get a more "objective" point of view?

The question is a "teaser." A psychiatrist like Sheri's was hardly objective in intimating that his own world-view was correct. There are bad Christian counselors and good secular ones. The point for the Christian is to sort out valid psychiatric insights from the perspective of the Christian faith.

8. Study these Scripture references. Are such passages applicable in any way in this situation? Ephesians 4:14; 1 Timothy 6:3–5; 2 Timothy 3:13; 4:3–4; 2 Peter 2:1.

Answers will vary. The texts do encourage us to be aware of world-views that are contrary to Christianity.

9. What should be Sheri's next step?

Back to the means of grace! Our Lord says: "Come, all you who are thirsty, come to the waters; and you who have no money, come, buy and eat! Come, buy wine and milk without money and without cost" (Isaiah 55:1).

Prayer

Lord, please get Your Holy Spirit going to thrust me out of myself to help others when I am "in the pits." Do it, Lord! Move me, Lord! Change me, Lord! Forgive me, most of all, for my self-centeredness and self-pity. I call on Your name, O Lord, for You have promised to hear me. And now, I *trust* You. I'm ready, Lord. I am waiting for You, Lord. In the strong name of Jesus Christ. Amen.

Hymn

"May We Your Precepts, Lord, Fulfill"

SESSION 5
Reaching Out

Stories

Let the People Say AMEN!
An "Exclusive" Church

For Discussion

The questions following the story—and subsequent vignettes—really call for personal opinions and self-probing of your own congregation's openness to strangers. Accordingly, no detailed guidelines are offered for the discussion leader at this point. However, you may wish to utilize this vignette:

On the CBS feature "Newsbreak," Charles Osgood commented on the efforts of a religion editor of one of the Cleveland papers who was conducting an ongoing experiment. Each Sunday this editor would anonymously visit one of the churches in the Cleveland area and give his evaluation of the service he attended.

Following the lead of people who assign stars to restaurants, this man judged the service in four categories—preaching, music, format and fellowship—attributing from one to three stars to each category.

After attending more than 22 such various services, he had given the top number of 12 stars to only two congregations. One was a black congregation and the other a Pentecostal store-front situation. In his commentary he was quoted as saying that the loneliest hour of the week may be reserved for a visitor entering a Christian church to join in worship and fellowship. He particularly criticized the "coffee hour" which followed the service and which usually left him standing by himself sipping his coffee while the members chatted with their friends. ("Inside Immanuel," newsletter of Immanuel Lutheran Church, Danville, CA, September 1978)

Christ invites all people to His banquet table. But do *we* welcome them?

Prayer

Give me the spectacles of Your Spirit, Lord, that I may see the world as it really is. Give me the grace to be *in* society while not succumbing *to* its values. Enable me to be Your agent—of truth and not compromise, of honest questions and not just dissent, of justice and mercy where there is prejudice and oppression. May I be a "little Christ," Lord. In the strong name of Jesus Christ. Amen.

Hymn

"Blest Be the Tie That Binds"

Love and Aging

Story

The Lover

For Discussion

1. What struck you most about this story?
Answers will vary.

2. What insights did you gain from Lou Harkness's reminiscences?

The Apostle Paul wrote that when he was a child he spoke as a child (1 Corinthians 13:11). But hopefully we all mature and see the follies and foibles of our youth from an adult perspective. You may wish to probe Lou's distinction between "infatuation" and *lasting* love—and how we can help youth to recognize the difference.

3. As life changes, and we (hopefully) mature, our perceptions shift. The "loves" of the past are seen from a distance. We recall different "loves." The greatest incarnation of love is God Himself. Study these Scripture passages and compare them to the common, often superficial, uses of the word *love*. God's love: John 3:16; Romans 5:7, 8; Ephesians 2:4–5; 1 John 3:1. Our love toward God: Deuteronomy 6:5; 2 Thessalonians 3:5; Jude 21. Love toward others: Matthew 22:39; John 13:34, 35; 15:12; 1 Peter 1:22. And note that the great "Love Chapter," 1 Corinthians 13, really begins with 1 Corinthians 12:31b.

Have individuals or small groups of 3 or 4 each research

one of the 3 kinds of love and then report their findings. *God's love*—unlike merely human love, it reaches out to save even the unlovable. *Our love toward God*—it is intended to encompass all our being, and is powered by God's love for us in Christ. *Love toward others*—again, it is powered by God's love for us in Christ.

4. An "in" word these days is *bonding*. A mother "bonds" with her child, a father with his son, spending "quality" time in deepening and enriching their relationship. In some areas, even in Christian congregations, a man or woman may "bond" with a person of the opposite gender who is not their spouse. It is understood that the relationship is purely platonic (intellectual and social) without *any* romantic involvement. There is simply a deep common sharing of mutual interests and the nurture of a fine Christian friendship. What do you think of this trend?

The author believes that this is the devil's workshop. See 1 Corinthians 10:12.

Story

The Romantic

For Discussion

1. Is Art Wright an "old fool"?

No. He "has it all together." He knows the reality of deep, lasting, *unconditional commitment*. And note that the base of their dedication to each other was their "strongly sharing the Christian faith in which they were married." Do statistics tell anything? Consider the following from the U.S. Census Bureau:

> Although nationally one out of two marriages currently ends in divorce, those who have church weddings and attend church regularly beat the odds by one in 50. But of couples who have married in the church, attend church regularly, *and* have family worship, one in 1,105 ends in divorce.

2. Is "love at first sight" possible? Is it wise?

Some long-married couples may have "known" it was

"forever" soon upon meeting. (This author "knew" within three weeks—and has been married, at this writing, for 45 years.) But "love at first sight" can also be a momentary fascination—as in "The Lover."

3. "Beauty is only skin deep." What do you think is the real basis of Art and Julia's relationship?

Certainly it is first of all their common Christian faith. Secondly, it's their unfailing love as they *age*. Third, they've kept their sense of humor!

4. Do we ever live with false idealizations of the opposite sex?

Of course we do. Help the group probe what these are and what individuals *first of all* desire in a spouse or friend.

5. Is the idea of "one person in the world for me" realistic? Is it self-serving?

Hopefully the Christ-man/Christ-woman desires to "be faithful unto death" to one's marital partner. But we fail often. Divorce can result. Dreams are shattered. But the ideal of "I pledge thee my troth until death us do part" is *not* intrinsically *self*-serving.

6. Does God have a "plan" for our lives? How does the Christian find out what "God's plan" may be? A young seminary student said this: "If the good Lord wants me to get married, He knows my address: Concordia Seminary, St. Louis, Missouri." How does the Christian know the difference between "waiting on the Lord" (Psalm 27) and taking action on one's own?

"Waiting on the Lord" is a response of trust *after* one has taken action, not "on ones own," but prayerfully asking for God's guidance in the action taken.

7. What are the clues to "a love that never ends"? See 1 Corinthians 12:31; 13:13; Ephesians 5:21–29; Colossians 3:19; 1 Peter 3:1.

Christ's love for us is the model and *power* that enables us to love others. That kind of love is not dominating, abusive, arrogant; but selflessly reaches out for the good of the other.

8. Does this story have any relevance for divorced people? For persons who are single?

Answers will vary.

Prayer

Give me the long-range view, O Lord, the eternal perspective of preparing for the life to come in Your presence and yet living each day here and now for itself. Make me mindful of past blessings and content with Your plan for my life today. As I watch and pray daily for Your return, may I never live in fear or anxiety but always in joyful anticipation of the grandest family reunion of them all. In the strong name of Jesus Christ. Amen.

Hymn

"Guide Me, O Thou Great Jehovah"

ACKNOWLEDGMENTS

About This Book
J. Russell Hale was quoted by Donald L. Deffner in *The Compassionate Mind: Theological Dialog with the Educated* (St. Louis: Concordia Publishing House, 1990), pp. 37–38.

Session 2
"Don't You Like My Present?" appeared originally in *This Day* 15:22 (August 1964), copyright © 1964 by Concordia Publishing House. All rights reserved.

Session 5
"An 'Exclusive' Church" is from Donald Deffner, *Seasonal Illustrations for Preaching and Teaching* (San Jose, CA: Resource Publications, Inc., 1992), pp. 75–76. Used by permission.

Session 6
"The Romantic" appeared originally in *The Lutheran Witness* 111:8 (August 1992), copyright © by Donald L. Deffner.

Also my thanks go to Christina Wolff, David Owren, Earl Gaulke, and the Educational Development staff of Concordia Publishing House, and to Jessica Wilmarth for her usual outstanding work at the computer.